Impressions

Impressions

...Sharing the Human Experience

Cora Davis

Library of Congress Control Number: 2021917562

PAPERBACK: 978-1-955955-75-1
EBOOK: 978-1-955955-76-8

Ordering Information:

For orders and inquiries, please contact:
1-888-404-1388
www.goldtouchpress.com
book.orders@goldtouchpress.com

Printed in the United States of America

Contents

Part 1: The Individual

Part 2: The Concept

Part 3: The Group, Survival

Dedication

This book is dedicated to parents and their children of ages twelve and up.

In each endeavor of our lives, we are encouraged by others and by our own inner strengths to improve, to endure. Obviously, parents have first claim to inspire the direction their children's lives take. Others enhance and help to advance that direction towards progress.

What a powerful role parents have as guides to bond, to prepare, to nurture, to inspire!

Here's to all of you who impart the best of yourselves to give to others!

Introduction

The poems assembled for this book are of diverse subjects and many of the verses may relate to each other only as poems. They blend many of the themes, concepts and experiences that cause individuals to share the human experience.

It is hoped that IMPRESSIONS will provide interesting reading and in some instances inspiration and information. The subjects and style are varied. Many of the poems contain rhyme and rhythm because those devices seem to appeal to many young readers. Also, a variety of reading levels are included because one level fits all does not apply to all readers of the same age group.

In the first section, Part One: The Individual, where specific characters narrate, the characters or voices are fictionalized representations. Some include children or parents, male or female speakers confronted with questions of individuality, maturing, or assisting with growth or of facing adjustments to life's challenges. The focus is on the realization of shared experience, of learning to value intangible treasures, to solve problems, to harbor patience, to cope with and to let go at appropriate times, to appreciate perspectives and outlooks that encourage growth and, or convictions, to inspire the connections that sustain successful development. Being a part of conversations that may influence a successful life beyond one's own lifetime could be a priceless gesture.

In Part Two: The Concept, the poems relate many of the ideas that individuals explore during efforts to contend with difficulties, to examine and evaluate possibilities, to appreciate the human bond. The aim is not to simplify weighty issues, but to focus on realities in a manner that may inspire some measure of appreciation or comfort, or, to suggest an idea not yet pondered. Since ideas and decisions are often formed after observing the frailties, mistakes or successes by those who have precedence, the youthful observer has an opportunity to form plans that could avoid mishaps that could consume too much space in his or her life. Discussions on a wide range of subjects are included in this section.

In Part Three, The Group: Survival, one poem takes glimpses at one of the many groups of people whose narratives comprise the story of America. This poem takes a brief look at the journey of African Americans from the stealthy ocean voyage, through endurances of emotional turmoil, at the bleak experiences of "coping," at the contributions and gains of a beleaguered people who often have born single, negative, ubiquitous descriptions assigned to the whole group. The reader gets a peek at how different individuals respond to and compensate for or with struggles in different ways. More than two generations have passed since federal legislation was enacted to rectify many of the lingering wrongs extended to race and gender. This narrative attempts to relate through verse parts of a conundrum of activities that chronicle this American story. The poem was written 1996.

Further reading for a more complete history would be beneficial for all Americans of this and other immigrant stories as information about all groups of people fosters understanding and broadens perspectives. Readers are encouraged to make personal lists of references offered by public libraries or by book stores for more information on this and other stories of American immigrants.

All of the poems in this collection may not be for all ages. The goal is that the poems will be used for discussion.

PART ONE

The Individual

In the Grand Scheme of Things

I am you
and you are me.
Our basic functions are universal,
but we are set in a different place and position
in the cosmos.

My vision
encompasses a distinction in the
aspects of the order and system of things,
not necessarily through shaded or uncurtained windows,
but from a unique point
you cannot occupy
because my space, like yours,
houses one tenant.

Glimpses of the impact
of chromosomal influences,
of what has passed by or gone through the windows, or
of what has been thrust upon us
can be interpreted, but
can never be understood completely
as our compositions and our
orbital paths are unprecedented.
Memory and documentation are sieved.

We are each other
because we need identification and unity.
But, we cling to
compacted influences,
personal experiences and
intimate outlooks
that make each of us who and what we really are.

The Camel

Passing Through the Eyes of Wonder

It was just sitting there –
that brownish yellow and green-trimmed
chunk of china, a formation of a kneeling camel
that had been in our family
long before my arrival.
It had maintained its
chiseled, pleasing, hollow structure
without scrapes or fractures.

I had often looked
at its long, powerful neck and
at its mournful, sloping face
featuring expressive, eyelashed eyes
and wondered what it would have seen and heard if
life had been breathed into its sculptured image
and it had become animated and verbal.

Perhaps its big, flat feet would have been
lonely for piles of Arabian sand,
for deserts,
for passengers in turbaned headdress
waiting to board its blanketed saddle,
and for a balking companion
to share things dromedary.

Maybe it could have told me
stories of America in decades past –
about the gay 1890's
or the roaring twenties.
Maybe it would have heard
the jubilant sounds
on the farms, in small towns, or in the cities
at the end of World War II.

Or, maybe it could have told me about
the different houses that had been called home,
about family gatherings,
about idiosyncrasies of family members …
about the things that made my relatives laugh,
that made them sad,
or gave them hope.

And when it had finished
all of the details,
all of the stories,
about all of the things I had not known,
I would have felt a bonding
and a rich, warm kinship
that would have been unbreakable.

Oops! No! No!
Now it's broken!
Is the link to my past broken too?

One Month in November

Twenty years have passed.
But, I remember it still.
Time crept by like a tired turtle
as my sister and I –
she, a fourteen-year old, creepy, skinny girl
and I, a twelve-year old, brainy, muscular boy –
waited for that defining phone call
that would deliver
the potentially harrowing, life-altering words.

We took turns
sitting on the short, multi-stripped sofa
and in the big, cushy chair
next to the telephone in the living room
during that appointed time:

"… between 5 and 6 P.M.
the week of Thanksgiving.
I will call."

The note had left echoes in my head.

As we sat at our posts
feigning homework but
daydreaming and replaying scenes of happier days of
tussling with our parents on the living room carpet,
bouncing the ball, alone or in frantic competition,
        on the cemented square in the back yard,

roaming in the woods collecting rocks
     for the garden wall,
being the one honored to safeguard tickets
     for special events and exciting places,
while our respective, mirrored thoughts,
     interrupting auditorily now and then,
were stuck in rewind.
And so was time.

We wondered what we had done wrong,
and each blamed the other …
naming senseless pranks
and not measuring up to scripted expectations.

The four days passed like weeks
until that fateful shrill
stopped the replay!

And my sister and I
reached for the phone simultaneously!
Our motions and emotions were frozen on pause
until we heard Dad's words:
"No divorce! I'm coming home!"

Rambling Memories

How sad it would have been to have missed those times with hours to while away:
loitering and chatting with friends and making rules to suit dawdling play,
watching boisterous friends settle scores of spats with loud words and knuckles,
or, with arm in arm, firmly forcing one's strength 'til the loser buckles...

Playing homemade board games, ball games, or any kind of competition match,
stopping at the scheduled time to rush home to savor food cooked from scratch,
eating with family and sharing selected stories of the day,
doing assigned chores at home and helping next door neighbors without pay...

Biding my time dreaming and waiting for magical birthdays to come,
listing limits and ultimatums, things I wanted to escape from;
but, distance and time have made sentimental memories of the past –
pleasant, indelible recollections that will undoubtably last.

How regrettable it would have been not to have had those times at all
or, to have had all inclinations granted at every beck and call.
How fortunate to have explored my environs safely and carefree
and, to have such special people remain a permanent part of me.

Learning Hard Lessons

The steep hill was the final challenge
to prove that big brothers
were true biking champs.

Sitting proudly on the seat
with hands firmly grasping
the shiny, ridged handle bars,

he bent his legs appropriately
and placed his feet securely
on the pedals

then arched himself above his seat
with his back angled
somewhat like a falcon ready to collect his prey.

A steady gaze at the road was the final act
before pushing down
to feel the surge of power

that sent the two wheeler
rolling over the narrow dirt road
hardened and smoothed by road scrapers.

Showing off with one hand
waving victoriously in the air
then graduating to no hands holding

were well-rehearsed skills
that had proved his readiness
for the awesome test: the big hill.

Finally, the right time had come.
The warm, still air was consoling,
and in the audience of one, an idolizing cherubic face beamed!

This was the moment
to display his expertise, to make an enviable and lasting impression.

The thrill itself stood forefront
dominating all else until
the bottom of the rugged hill

seemed to loom upwards, like a backhoe, met the dazzled biker
with a whopping smack, rendered him a broken leg
and left him with a harsh realization:

Control is a possessive, gripping skill
requiring full attention,
demanding respect and restraint.

Stepping into Another World

There she is playing dress up
in full-blown adult garb
and in make-up replete with
headdress and accessorized ears and eyes.

What fun it is
to visit the grown up world.
to pretend to be there
while strutting on an illusionary runway,
to answer imaginary questions
about real things,
to put on an imitable, shiny tiara,
to cry whimsical tears of joy,
to exit a mock stage and glide
among fanciful admirers
in a make-believe audience!

What a stark contrast
to her existence of one decade
and to the realm of calamity
embracing her last four seasons

where bitter events of severity have
painted indelible pictures of hardship:

of blasts of gunfire echoing among city sounds,
of victims of misfortune lying in heaps of rubbish,
of confused fancies jumbling give and take,
of stopgap places called home, of making do and making it without

and where discarded objects
gain new status as welcomed, comforting manna!

Unexpected Kindnesses

Good evening, little kitty cat.
Are you lost or do you live nearby?
Has your family fed you today?
Would you like a piece of pumpkin pie?
Here, Kitty! Here Kitty! Have a bite.
Oh, come on, Kitty. It's quite okay.
Should you be out all alone at night?
Must you go? Do you have time to stay?

There, there, Kitty, have some milk.
This crystal cup is pretty and nice
but it is not too special for you.
If you have no home, may I entice
you to stay right here, to choose this place.
Or, will pumpkin pie and milk not do?
Is that a smile on your furry face?
If you are pleased, I am happy too.

Ah, little one, you're turning to go …
But, with a warm, full tummy, I hope.
Thanks for chasing the shadows away.
Come back to see me another day.
Goodbye! Goodbye, kitty cat! Stay kind.
Bye! I hope your family won't mind!

Mentoring

Reflections from Pro to Minor

Once I reached for the clear blue sky
and saw all of my dreams come true.
I laughed and sang and played with toys
and did the things that most kids do.
I wrestled and scrapped like other boys
and dared the improbable too.

Once I sat on the sideline bench
waiting to hear the words, "Play ball!"
Then up I'd jump and off I'd run
as part of my team's defense wall.

Once my joy was in competing
and trying and winning blended.
In each match the game was the thing
no matter how the play ended.
But, winning brought a special zing
that left goofs and errors mended.

Life was quite simple then, but now that I have grown
where dreams once grew, seeds of uncertainty are sown.
Where songs once dwelled, dejection is an intrusion.
Laughter is often lost in foolish confusion.

The time that play consumed is loaded with labor.
Playing is too great a luxury to savor.
Real success waits patiently with reservation.
Taking risks is defended by hesitation.

But, everything is not depressing in this phase.
There are glimpses of joy and achievement, most days.
Reality includes blows and complications.
The strategy is balance and moderations.

And so, my friend, in your heart keep these thoughts sublime:
Control impulses. Enrich your gifts. Treasure time.

Womanhood in the Making, A Mother's Quest

We are learning together, my daughter and I,
of six sets of traits to construct her future by.
A look at where we stand reveals the progress
of growth and efforts made and needs we must address.

Her honesty and integrity –
suffering a few bruises here and there
from broken promises, half truths
and tangled tales revealing immaturity –
have been resurrected
and are developing well.
But, she is so trusting.

So, how do I forewarn or attempt to certify
the existence of camouflaged, paper heroes
who will surely give her heart and her trust a try?

The basic ingredients for her intelligence and foresight
appear and disappear
as hormonal balances and judgement seek alignment,
shifting in various directions
as pressures are applied.
But, she has a remarkable mind!

Yet, how do I regulate, steer or motivate
a questioning, wonderfully inventive mind
that will peer through rules, oppose, defy or create?

Her goals and aspirations
are blowing in the wind
threatening to land on uncertain sites
propped up by fantasy, whims and reveries
affected by a myriad of interests and unmasked talents.
No, she is not ready to alight.

What can I do to encourage and to ensure
that her present and future goals, aims and causes
settle on values and treasures that will endure?

Her courage and strength,
existing in a fertile genetic mixture,
sprout from an inner fortitude
that has seen her through near fatality
and through optional physical and social dares.
And, yes, she is so stubborn!

How should I try to discipline, curb or delay
a headstrong, determined, spirited attitude
that aims to be adventurous, to have its way?

There is no doubt
that she has an unhesitating and an unconstrained ability
to bond with people – both strangers and friends –
as her free and easy smile,
topped by ardent, transparent eyes, is a welcome mat.
But, her caring and kindness could be troubling clogs.

Will she falter, ignore or be quick to reveal
smoke screens and simulators and merciless fakes
who may try to take advantage of her good will?

The delicate, sometimes perplexing duty
of checking on these imperative building blocks
is sometimes mortifying, always challenging and
often appears to be an insurmountable task.
But, our beliefs and our faith rest on a firm foundation.

When her endeavors and beliefs have been tested
and problems are exhausting, I hope she will turn
to the God in which her faith has been invested.

I must make sure she knows that I believe in her
and that we both use knowledge and skills to deter
deficiencies, impediments and abuses
that could threaten or invite needless excuses.

And so, we accept our charge, my daughter and I,
to mature and to enjoy our ventures,
to use this opportunity,
the treasures and the challenges of each day,
to build productive, happy tomorrows.
Yes, our respective growths are falling in place.

Bobby Cougaran Plus Cay Brown

Bobby Cougaran sits under the big elm tree recalling the day
that he carved the initials BC+CB on the tree to stay.
Since that time CB has left town, BC is alone and times have changed.
For both, aspirations and priorities have now been rearranged.

How sweet it is to reminisce about innocent times spent alone
when a whole world of developing visions were hitherto unknown,
when paths untraveled waited for firm feet to make unique impressions
and thoughts, not yet mused, waited to occur in rational successions.

CB and BC shared their first kiss under these spreading dense branches –
a tender, shy expression filled with love and emotional fancies.
Drenched in wonder, warmth and certainty and totally free of guile,
they thought of themselves as inseparable, not as in single file.

Attending community and school affairs, they became the ideal –
models of loyalty and trust, their match was not virtual, but real.
Their shared extroverted activities roused the envy of their friends.
Their petty differences inevitably led to sound amends.

But, their outlook took a turn the day they heard a political speech!
Cay Brown was convinced to negate their dreams which came to a halting screech!
Inspired to lend a helping hand to unfortunate, desolate souls,
she reconsidered her well-intentioned plans, and then revised her goals.

Spurred on by sacrifice and good will as the drawbridge was raised that day –
forcing old dreams into murky waters as Bobby watched near the bay –
Cay Brown wiped her tears, braced her shoulders, waved good-bye and sailed towards the unknown.
Then Bobby, ignoring his streaming tears, faced the wooded path … alone.

... And Then Came Answers

On this roof,
in this secure, special place
are immutable memories
of age-old, generational agonies
explored and rehashed here –
here where Naiveté and earnest aims reigned.

In spring
Adolescence, clad in green and white
and covered with queries,
found this place
isolated from blurred pictures,
muffled explanations
and cryptic, indistinct responses.

Admittedly,
the ears and the eyes were closed to outsiders;
miscommunications caused clarity
to be muted and veiled.

Perversity –
bent on charting a new course,
on finding some measured adventure
hidden in intricate,
personal and mysterious caches
that only Youth could cipher –

went head strong
into a wilderness and into a civilization
with both detours and charted directions clearly labeled.
But, Youth had its way
seeking sequined excitement and fervid discoveries,
using experiences and acquired knowledge
along the way
to identify, to understand.

At last
the cluttered pathways were cleared
of noxious obstructions –
vanity, pretense, hostility ….

Two decades ensued
before a wiser, gentler traveler –
in fading shades of summer
returned accompanied by Love, Hope and Charity –
returned to this secure, special place,
returned to realizations that those who had preceded Youth
had been right all along.

Hope in Hard Places

I have seen you there
under the expressway bridge
with your cast off bedding
and wrappings left from meals.

You look forlorn and empty
like missed opportunity,
like dried up dreams
and broken promises.

Sometimes you stand
with others waiting for a short-term job
and you read the want ads
while you wait.

Maybe this will be the day,
the day that things will change …
after this day's work,
after this day's pay.

But, that was yesterday too.
What about tomorrow?
How long will you hope
before you throw away the want ads?

You Can Take Charge and Add Wings to Your Dreams

How can you dream, you ask
when meals are almost nonexistent,
when your roof is less than that
or when holes are the only things in your pockets?

You can dream for dreams are free!

You can dream
because dreams include the sky
and the air surrounding and sustaining your being,
because of the twinkle in your eye
and the smile on your face
inviting the same look in return.

You can dream because atmosphere is free!

You can dream
because you have roots
that connect the past
with the present and the future
with possibilities waiting to unfold
in the images that you control.

You can dream because imagination is free!

You can dream
because hope springs
from wells of inspiration
filled with belief
in your dominance over unending errors,
in your ability to reach, to grasp, to hold ...

You can dream because hope and faith are free!

You can dream
because you control the vigor and the ability
to set in motion
upright, creative ideas
that can fly, stand, endure
and reward your inner being.

You can dream because you exist to dream, to think, to accomplish!

Innocence... Disappeared

Was it lost among rows of daily strangers' cots
while attention played havoc with the future lots
of dozens of squirming, helpless, whining charges
kept in questionable, temporary lodges?

Was it lost in audio visual glitter
or among childhood rumpus and careless litter
where developing feelings were tumbled about,
while the idols of guidance wore faces of doubt?

Was it lost among forlorn sounds of pleas and shouts
when caring and receiving posed engaging bouts
placing temperaments and needs in mute conflict
as accountable guardians were lax, not strict?

Was it lost on playgrounds where frenzied bullies reigned?
Or, was it where discipline and interest waned
as understanding, hope and trust remained remiss
while violence produced an alarming abyss?

Was it lost when faithful sentinels left their posts
and passed to all kinds of contemporary hosts
a chance to abet or peddle creative fun,
while needs were procured and essential work was done?

Was it lost while no apparent reason was known,
while selected seeds for good character were sown
and carefully tended hours were spent ensuring
that futures would be bright and values enduring?

From the Observation Post

Be patient with me
for like you,
I am not perfect.

Like you, I must face
both paper and steel ogres
that challenge noble intents

by scouting for defenseless contents,
for risky ventures and
for waterborne foundations

through which to open pores
to weaken controls
of substance and character.

Like you, I must
post guards to watch
for both silent and glittering temptations

that slip through ranks
when sentinels are enfeebled
by penetrating or appealing agents

or when varying desires and needs
pose inevitable battles
alternating outcomes.

And, so the continuous conflicts ensue
interlacing, modifying, revitalizing and
providing stimulated resolve

to control, to subdue, to sober imperfections
as confidences spiral towards wise choices
or loom towards occasional lunacy.

Which Way? Straight Ahead Or Exit?

There in your vaulted room
with the luxury of time to think,
will thoughts of the past,
left uncordoned,
crowd and push to the forefront?
Will your present needs navigate meditation and
dominate day to day survival?
Or, will thoughts of your future
cascade over rumbling ghosts
to be heard?

When that unyielding door clung shut
and you were left alone in your single enclosure,
were you haunted
by visions of Herculean dominance,
of defenseless, selected victims, or
of shielded combatants
scrounging for continued breath?

Was the taste of triumph
a savored subsidized loot
or a daring social nectar?

When your contemporaries enter your presence,
are they in awe of your victories?
Do they welcome your entry
into a distinctive brotherhood?
Or, are there those who shun or fear
your pervading atmosphere?

Are your emotions illusive?
Do you hide your feelings behind a frozen front?

In your private moments,
when intrusive housemates are engaged elsewhere,
do shadowy giants from childhood dreams
or from perceptive visions of what might have been
invade, encroach and limit?
Do thoughts of the lane not taken
suffocate or enlighten?

In those quiet times of sanity,
can you feel the presence of a directive power
positioned at exit ramps
pointing to the high road?
Or, is the view blocked by bullying glutonous ogres
beckoning you straight ahead or below?

If you scramble to overpower
the extra baggage of weighty burdens,
or of past wrongdoings,
can you conceive a locale where mistakes exist, but
grace and goodness rule
because trust and faith abide
to quell unsettling egos?

When that final gate is locked
from the other side,
will a detour change the direction?
Or, will there be full throttle ahead
down a twilight zone
that returns to that unyielding door?

Letting Go

My daughter has packed her bags
to take on a momentous journey
through passages of exciting collegiate adventures
where challenges will temper her impressive capabilities,
where dares will test her vulnerabilities,
where invitations to squander time await
to attempt to finagle detours, and
where Independence and Determination
will become entities and escorts.

She can never return to this place
where rows of soft, spongy sentries
kept the dragons away,
where she entertained chimerical visitors
from enchanted lands,
where timbered beams were formed,
where strokes of endearment were always nearby
to direct, protect and sometimes coddle,
where her gingerly monitored activities inspired pride
and occasionally triggered tense anxiety
as she blossomed and sometimes faltered.

Now it is time to pull back on the yoke
and let her rise to try her wings
and gain a breadth of knowledge and experiences
that will allow her
to soar through tranquil skies
and to survive brawling turbulences.

And, at a time
the future now holds,
she will stand
during her personal intermission
in this place
where I now pause
to release and let go.

Faith in the Invisible Nods

He is the Adonis and the Owens and the sage
that I admired
when I was his age.
I aspired to be both
the versatile athlete and the scholar.
But, reality urged me to strive for the later
and to be an onlooker for the former.

His mind and his body coordinate
his impressive attributes.
His dexterity is complimented
by broad skills and interests
developed by fusions of
diligent encouragement, persistent requirements
and his own menus
of fascinations and finesse.

His successes often make him a magnate
for those seeking to share the light
cast by his athletic victories
and by his mind boggling chess triumphs.

The need to scrutinize,
to delay, to prepare,
to be selective, to abstain
are choices he must continue to make
before treading in potentially perilous territories,
before charting a future
now existing in the blind spots.

We have the big talks,
he and I,
with silence dotting my pauses.
After the last session,
he interrupted
the final quiet space.

"Don't worry, Dad. I hear you
before you utter a word.
I listen to your counseling
long after the talking is done.
You take the spoils."

PART TWO

The Concept

Bravo!

One lone star,
blocked by a silent cloud,
waiting for its moment of pleasure,
dazzles and glitters
though there is no measure
of its performance,
no applause for its éclat,
its striking effect.
Unceremonious attention
unclaims its spectacular act.

Jarred Back to Reality

She was standing there with her whole world at her feet.
Her worn, leather, zippered bag was parked on the street.
Alongside the suitcase, a red shopping bag stood
bearing posh logo from an uptown neighborhood.

Although her seedy, blue silk suit showed signs of wear,
it revealed the fitted trim of a tailor's care.
Her shoes, beginning to fray, were a perfect blend.
But the scowl on her face implied the need for a friend.

The first "Hello" reached ears closed to the active world.
Persistence brought jarred senses alert and unfurled.
As her cynical look faded into a smile,
she relaxed and exposed a charming, elegant style.

"Thank you for the friendly words," she calmly declared.
"Your warmth is something for which I was not prepared.
Most passersby seem to have grown callous and blind
seldom responding to the luckless and resigned."

Moving to a nearby bench in the city park,
she motioned for her new acquaintance … to embark
on a storied journey of life in hard places.
Then she revealed a tale of woe and absent graces:

Multiples of star-crossed ills and inept choices,
puerile management and impetuous voices
led the way through complicated propositions
through mazes that ended in abandoned missions.

Left with unfilled promises and bare coffers,
dreams without wings, fleeting friends and sterile offers,
she had nurtured incubated, afflicted hope
in mean, bleak, adverse places as she tried to cope.

This day, months after her fall, she felt a warm glow,
the melting of her frosted cover, and a slow
inner thawing of a spirit willing to dare
to compete again, to regain her former flair.

As she turned to face the gentle listener who
had entered her forsaken, cold world to imbue
a lost soul with a simple, "Hello, how are you,"
there was no trace of the stranger, no trail to ensue.

Incorporated

We are each unique embodiments of diverse investors –
our innate traits, external influences and ancestors –
together constructing a single being, one existence.

What a miraculous thing it is to be one of a kind:
to have choices, distinct possibilities and one's own mind,
to be able to dream, to grow, and to make a special mark
after discovering the impetus, the control, the spark
to arouse visions, to stir the spirit and to feed the soul.

If circumstances permit and appropriate growth ensues,
and if influences are supporting, then purpose imbues
dominoes of ideas and skills and achievements of goals
preparing the ambitious for fulfillment and starring roles
preparing all for personal measures of victory.

How fortunate to have such varied ancestry pave the way
leaving relics, monuments, and volumes of knowledge to stay
and to inherit institutions of order and mores
giving protection, shape, and inspiration in countless ways,
leaving tangibles and intangibles of infinite worth.

A unity of three continually urging, molding,
showing, instructing, impressing, empowering, unfolding
the primordial, original, transient you and me.

The Real Annie Marie

Annie Marie was but a shy, old-fashioned girl
like a rare, uncut diamond or rough-hewn pearl.
A mere glance disguised her unseen latencies,
gifts waiting to unfurl in eddied cadencies.

Like ponchos protecting the wearer from showers,
influence from the latest styles had no powers
to drench spirits already settled or assumed
for her vacuous life seemed already entombed.

She fancied no exciting or lavish existence
as she moved unpretentiously, without resistance
and without weighted expectances to befall
gathering no balks, amassing no wherewithal.

Simplicity and sheer honesty portrayed her style
without alluring, bold wrappings, deceit or wile.
Not seeking new ventures or desiring to dare,
she accepted life without flourishes or fanfare.

But, as circumstances often divert events,
scramble common images, or alter contents,
Annie, trying to evade a mall make-up technique,
was convinced to let "an artist" bare her "mystique."

Gently coaxed with gifts of necessities and ease,
she gave in, closed her eyes, and relaxed to appease
enthusiastic experts eager to convert
discordant segments to an amazing concert.

Shifting from moments of ethereal pleasure,
she paused to end the comfortable, soothing leisure.
Smiling mannequin-like faces veiled a secret
as her wondering eyes feared dismay and regret.

Minutes crept by as she waited to see the change
made by busied, hushed artists' amazing range.
Taunted and cajoled, her anticipation surged
'til relief was found as questions and answers merged.

Cast in the mirror was a countenance exposed
by four talented hands of loveliness reposed.
Awakened Venus-like beauty glowed with delight
attracting oglers pleased with the amazing sight.

"Never again," affirmed a soft, comforting voice,
"should you deprive yourself of this beautiful choice."
And so, with advice and encouragement, she vowed
to maintain the look with which she had been endowed.

Armed with wrappings concealing her inner being,
Annie charmed acquaintances who were not seeing
the formerly contented, pure, ungarnished face
that was at peace with unsophisticated grace.

But, after having blossomed with boldness and dash,
she displayed talents with craftiness and panache
revealing fields of artistic ripples and knacks,
attracting strong encouragement and mild attacks.

Encountering overtures to major pretense
when summoned to pose for misleading contents
of promises of a miracle preparation,
she became aware of an acute realization:

While it was pleasing to be admired for her façade.
the greater satisfaction with her lot was made
by recognition of her intrinsic virtues
which seemed cast as minor or subordinate clues.

Enriched by new and varied experiences
but disturbed by resulting interferences
with familiar images beneath the mirage,
she vowed to remove the adorning camouflage.

Of Heeding a Sui Generis {Unique} Calling

There is a place deep inside –
       a fantastic, ethereal, majestic cavern
       where exquisite, peaceful, furious wonders wait
a place where intrinsic thoughts abide –
       eerie, magnificent, awe-inspiring, fragile lumps
       awaiting delicate, passionate, powerful discharges –
a place where rooms of reveries dwell –
       a graduated, sensitive, labyrinthine abode
       seeking a creative, patient, fierce inhabitant –
a place where melodious sounds dwell –
       from sated, voracious nooks and crannies
       shielding imaginative, fanciful, prodigious creations -
a place housing a magnum opus
       designed exclusively for its keeper. It is a metier
       encased in a coffer requiring distinctive responses –
a chest exacting direct focus
       demanding indefatigable, ardent attention
resulting in a bra vura when developed talents mature.

The entrance through its noble portal,
       a gateway to many chambers is sometimes facile,
       frequently intricate, and too often never approached.
Yet, it is enclosed in each mortal,
       and, the endowments lodged on tiered levels,
when nurtured and expressed, compliment a brilliant creation.

When a magnetic throb makes contact,
       an electric, incisive, yet calming impulse
       with a restless, spirited craving explodes!
A raging, exciting, serene impact
       reveals the quenching of a thirsty ravenous art,
an extraordinary masterwork, unveiled.

Storing Hidden Moments of Pleasure

Adjusting time to fit the needs
of constant cares, woes and wants leads
to filled hours of both haste and waste.
Rushing to pick up, to carry ...
leaves too little time to tarry.

Making appointments to settle
ideas to boost the mettle,
to encourage the very best,
hoping to surpass, to outdo
leaves little time to miss a cue.

But arranging time to linger,
to pause ... now that is the clinger,
the thing, the time to seize, to take,
to make certain that each day's goal
includes joys that cling to the soul.

Among intangibles that last,
that mold tender imprints that cast
flowered curlicues on the heart,
are a child's laughter and soft smile,
a good friend's eyes and winning style.

Moments that matter here and there,
that lend a touch of love and care
will make a special difference
long after the time has gone by ...
to renew the natural high.

Of Liberty Concentrated Preparation and Instant Gratification

So very much alike and so varied we humans are
with our personalized lists of essential needs to bar
interference with our rights to liberty, as to hear
the same symphony of tunes, but not the same melody,
to choose the musicians and to adjust the harmony.

How patiently some arrange their notes
while developing and adjusting to demanding quotes
of appropriate prerequisites for accomplished goals,
delaying delights in simple and temporal pleasures
until all compulsions are in place for lasting treasures.

Discontent and restlessness claim those who refuse delay
who, like contenders in a race, must hasten to relay,
to finish segments, only laps of a measured distance;
but, unlike the revered runner, life's onrush continues
through arduous trials, obstacles, and daunting venues.

Indulging in glitter and glitz, things that Waste and Greed buy –
far removed from necessities, on things we can rely
before vital needs are met and foundations are confirmed –
stresses the misfortune of instant gratification
while pious values and basics dwell in renovation.

Of Invading Behaviors and Patriot Paragons

Oh, what a jumbled batch of misfortune we have allowed
to take root, produce, and become improperly endowed,
hardy, kudzued pollutions with toxic agitations
to diffuse fears and destructions without hesitations.

Prompt reminders leap from the media, lest we forget,
that poverty-stricken spirits are eager to abet,
to give impulse to pure or kindred souls, to perpetrate
acts of violence or vice that destroy or desecrate.

Firm notoriety claims appalling offenders who,
without apparent foresight, conscience, compassion or rue
commit malevolent, felonious, and callous acts
with little or no reflection for resounding impacts.

In the shadows of the spotlight quiet, patriot bees
plan, deliver, assist, comfort or support without fees
because neither fame nor fortune is the inspiration
that fosters the need for constant, humane dedication.

Flanked by employed service producers with similar goals,
dutiful spirit builders play indispensable roles.
Outnumbering culprits who peddle dread and cause grief,
Paragons wait off stage supplying care, hope and relief.

The Unhidden Truth

To its viewer the mirror reflects an image
of one of a kind in chronicled lineage
of an unduplicated, related, once-made
never to be repeated, blue printed façade.
A hint to what lies unexposed is in the eye
reflecting the truths that the soul cannot belie.

In day to day struggles to please and to succeed
the ordinary person proposes to lead
the customer, the patron, the client, the foe
to see, to believe what may or may not be so
relying on appearance for a desired end
employing camouflage to attract, to befriend.

The talented performer plays tricks with the eye.
As magician his dares never fail to defy
what is probable or possible, real or true,
what is within his reach or what he cannot do
relying on memory, distraction and speed
and delighting in proficient feints to mislead.

Convinced pretense is the successful actor's goal.
Yet, seeming is but a sandcastle to the soul –
temporary, impressive, artistic beauty
excelling in auspicious though fleeting duty –
but, like the flood or high tide, its power enraged,
the role ends! Change prevails. Truth emerges unstaged.

One of a kind, singular, whatever the role –
uniqueness of manner, talent, vision and soul –
traits that grant individuals a special mark,
that give the eyes a distinctive message or spark ….
The truth the eyes may alter or try to conceal
what the soul in quiet, hushed moments must reveal.

File Condensation

Two personal files of life experiences:
one symbolizes production and fulfillment –
atonement, honor, benevolent devotion.
The other embodies spent opportunity:
abused privilege, malevolent promotion.

The giant compilations are stacked in plain view.
most details are shielded from casual glances
discouraging interference and intrusion.
Accurate, impartial and conclusive contents
characterize the meticulous inclusion.

Only Omnipotence with enduring powers
of wisdom and intellect can edit changes:
obliterate, rearrange, restate or append.
God's approval is needed to honor pardons,
release from transgressions, or neutralize to amend.

The Old Home Place

The old house is vacant now and the roof is caving in.
The top resembles a sinking ship, sans captain, sans crew.
But, in its heyday, it served its family well, but then
seven restless, aspiring siblings – three boys, four girls – grew
attended school, married, and moved on to other quarters
while aging parents, stilled by the quietness of it all –
of refereeing spats among brawling sons and daughters –
of chauffeuring, of cooking big meals, and shopping at the mall,
of noisy holiday galas, gifts and smiling faces,
of visitors and neighbors and dates running in and out,
of packing the truck and the car for faraway places,
of consoling crushed dreamers sated with hope and doubt,
of extending best wishes and hugging happy winners –
were finally left alone … being … waiting, just waiting ….

A Questioning Quandary?

Surrounded by answers, but filled with
troubles and assorted afflictions
Looking, not seeing, hearing, not heeding,
not avoiding contradictions
Feeling, but not bestowing, touching
but not retaining the impact
of thinking clearly before suggesting, of selecting,
of moving to act
of multiplying mistakes, not grasping responses
or caring to know
that blaming others and reducing one's own effect
is a paltry show
of concern for posterity, for showered blessings
and their continued flow.

Now and Then

Now and then when days are long
and woes overwhelm your trust,
reach within to find a song
and sing 'til a sudden gust
from menacing clouds explodes
to wash your troubles away.

Now and then when days are short
and schedules are much too long,
call forth strengths of every sort
and fill your lungs with a song
of joy and warmth and pleasure
and watch your cares fade away.

Now and then when days are dark
and shadows cover your dreams
look within, recall a lark
and laugh 'til happiness streams
down your cheeks in waterfalls
to wash your worries away.

Now and then when days are bright
and things are going your way
go within, reserve the light
and use it another day
in times of sorrow and gloom
to sweep your troubles away.

Behind the Clouds Motley Linings of Joy and Gloom

The rain came down in sheets softening the cracked earth
soaking seared spaces, changing rue to joy and mirth,
erasing the drought and replenishing the thirst.
But, when angry clouds exploded, a sudden burst
sent spates of pent up billows racing and razing!

The long-awaited pleasure from the parched abyss
became instead a search for protection, not bliss.
The angry torrents abrupted streams and widened rivers.
Havens became pervaded objects with quivers
of unsteadiness alarming fortunate survivors.

As clouds dissipated and gray skies became blue,
as darkness surrendered to daylight's baring hue,
revelations of nature's adjustments brought cries
of shocked reality and bewildered replies!
The soaring power of the rainstorm was made clear.

The awesome needs to grasp, to cope, and to rebuild
became the immediate desires to be filled –
desires that outweighed self-pity and loss of trust,
emotions that overshadowed doubt and disgust
for showers of another sort rushed in … Rescue!

But, Impatience, a creeping, impeding Stalker,
captured survivors who, unlike a pole vaulter,
failed to leap over all impediments, and plunged ...
falling victim to frenzied, rushed, hapless plans lunged
as help, but not benefitting the flooded prey.

Repulsive scavengers seeking personal gains
sought to profit from damages and victims' pains,
increasing demands to remain calm and alert,
requiring caution and the aptness to assert,
to defend against disingenuous transactions.

Helping hands from vested functions, strangers and friends –
empathetic with troubles that tragedy rends –
reached out extending concern, care, relief and hope,
helping victims to remain vibrant and to cope ...
receiving motley colors in the clouds' linings.

Never Alone

The wind is whistling,
but we're not.
The gusts are blasting southward
while we're heading northward
looking for a warm place to sleep.

The day was long,
but time was short
so all ends were not connected.
When the sun set,
we were not.

One more mile
and we'll be there.
Or, will we be there?
The inn may be full,
but we're not.

What happens, you ask,
if luck runs its course,
vacates our presence
and leaves us all alone?
We're not.

Ah, Patience!

Time creeps while contentions and agonies persist.
Waiting becomes an inhibiting catalyst.
Holding on becomes an unsettling focus.
Dwelling there is a strong force, an extra onus.

But, time is required for set patterns to unmold.
Cycles must evolve as intended to unfold.
We need to abide while a pearl becomes a pearl.
It takes years of encrustation, not one quick swirl.

Waiting is unwelcomed for many who hurry.
But, Time forms a basis and lessens the worry.
The builder waits for the engineer to survey;
for knowledge can allay or prevent dismay.

Patience is a bulwark and an enduring friend.
It is a benign stress that helps to apprehend.
What is best to come forth may not always seem so.
Eventually, all is clear and apropos.

The Power of Time

I faced an embattled truth today.
a stored reality locked away.
It had been too risky to unloose,
too fierce to tempt silenced emotions.
At last, there is no need to appease.
It is controlled, restrained and at ease.

Dormancy has calmed the wanderlust
and made it easier to adjust.
The truth, now unruffled and mellow,
is clear and insightful, not stifling.
Retrospection now moves without fear.
It is comforting, precious and dear.

Acceptance has relieved the anguish,
emotions that can impoverish
a spirit longing to be released
of tiptoed thoughts and guarded desires,
challenges to destiny's design.
Accepting is wise, warm and benign.

Wisdom ferments before it is done.
It endures throes, woes and contention.
Life's encounters fill its huge caldron
with broad ranges of sadness and joy.
Time passes and diverse mixtures blend
yielding seasoned thoughts that comprehend.

Surviving Dreams

This is not the dream you pined for
when you lay under the elm with books for a pillow.
That dream had bells that rang with gusto
and had lights that glowed like sparkling neons
attracting gold, fame and laughter.

This dream must have been transposed
from some other place into this other likeness
whose image is deceptive triumph
with wailing bells like distant sirens
and with blinking lights triggered by misfortune.

Did sparkling, regal neons lose their luster
and modify your aims to soar …
somewhere in crowded, secluded valleys
or on steep, jagged mountain tops
where more appealing visions gleamed?

Change, life's skulky, inevitable nemesis
waiting, demanding to be summoned,
must have intervened with its monstrous grace
to transport you to this seemingly unlikely place
where rewarding dreams survive in lean subsistences.

Man in the Park

Wrinkles, like crumpled linen,
    covered his weary, calloused face.
pudgy, dripping nose
    centered between wan, sallow, sagging cheeks,
fading, dim eyes
    shaded by brows having known a former grace ….
Atop this tousled, gray, hairy heap,
    a furrowed forehead peaks.
His crowning glory, like blotched thinning grass
    blowing in the breeze
danced to and fro as he tried to nab his hat,
    but could not seize.
As if by request, a leafless limb
    cradled the crumpled cap.
Fidgety fingers slowly lifted
    the worn, blue head topper,
and he placed it, a proud Braves relic,
    lovingly on his lap.

The Last Good Bye

I was not there
as you lay dying
while you were contemplating
your last breath.

Entering that last unknown
must have been a lonely, apprehensive thing –
not terrifying, not threatening
but, lonely still.

Opening and closing that defenseless door
was a one-time act
with no audience except it.
It must have stood there hovering ….

It, that soft, quiet, powerful thing,
Death,
waiting to do its duty
whether or not there was a comforting wave
or, anyone to bid farewell.

The Final Garment

So short a time to complete the final garment.
So brief the span of our activity on earth –
one lifetime to qualify an insured warrant
of grace, good deeds, good intentions, good cheer and mirth.

Each stitch in the vestment depicts a chosen deed.
Every seam is a finished segment of the whole.
All of the tiered connections do somehow concede
that minute details are important to the role.

Every person is a featured solo player.
Each actor flaunts an incomplete identity
in a lifetime assigned to perfect each layer
as the production will last for infinity.

The colors for the custom-designed garment blend
to create the unique image of its bearer
as the robe and the actions help to comprehend
the worth of the exiting wearer.

PART THREE

The Group, Survival

Glimpses of the African Americans' Journey, An American Story

Once upon a time Hope became a dark, distant, melancholy mystery
for woeful, African captives shuffled into a distressing history
by fellow humans whose desires for wealth and ease were terribly misguided
as they seized reluctant, future toilers whose humanity was derided.
So, a story of horror, shame, agony and divested decency began.

The long, dreadful, ocean voyage carted trapped, frightened, crestfallen people who –
walled in by brine, misery, filth, enmity, brutality and sounds of grief – grew
wearier and wearier fighting Despondency who, at times, lost its grip
casting some overwhelmingly sad captives from its hold as they leapt from the ship
that sailed dejectedly on towards a benighted, uncertain, uncharted fate.

Debarking brought no relief as hostile hosts waiting ashore assured bondage
by greeting questioning, confused faces, not with brotherly love, but umbrage
and opposition to their requests for freedom, deliverance, care and ease.
Foreign voices resisted the unwanted mission and tried to appease
their wounded spirits while they moaned separation from family and homeland.

As passing days mounted into weeks, resistance made life abrasive and hard.
So, outward courage faded as Submission doubled as Comforter and Guard
while enduring offensive acts, suffering physical blows, but retaining dreams –
dreams of freedom, visions of home – of things held in high esteem, and fleeting gleams
of rational thought when time allowed or sluggish stupor waned.

Adjusting to and coping with ruinous hardship to achieve a master's goal
became the somber focus of daily life, a disconsolate, daunting role
of spiritless labor, of assassinated talents, of wasted visions ....
Therefore, plans of escape and rebellion were bound to lead to bold decisions;
for Freedom is a huge thing, an invigorating, soul-hugging, steel desire.

Misplaced "property" – abducted, fled on its own accord – whatever the cause
left "owners" anxious to retrieve claims by resorting to runaway slave laws.
And, slaves resorted too through friends of slaves, underground railroads and coded song
to risk following Freedom's Star, to taste sweet Liberty and place it among
their most precious possessions ... a chance to envision, to breathe ad libitum.

As the struggles for territorial powers ensued, states' rights were cited.
But, when the Civil War ended, the North prevailed; the nation "united."
During the war, countrymen fought countrymen, some slaves included in dire strife,
procuring the country's unity with its most valuable resource: Life.
Change, War's resulting offspring, became a roving Astraea seeking sanity.

An enactment, the Constitution, presented the nature, limits and functions
providing what was needed to protect citizens, to enforce injunctions.
Unfortunately, lynchings, Jim Crow and slanted legal interpretations
hindered the slaves progeny from full savor of Freedom's realizations.
Slavery, no longer sanctioned, nor condoned, had left a haunting legacy.

Most former slaves and masters alike did not dismiss with the turn of a page
such powerful inflictions, economic changes, or for some restrained rage.
But, unlike avenger John Wilkes Booth or hooded, lynching Klansmen who exploded,
most began to hold respect for the noble intents of government and coded
responses to reality with blind or mute acceptance of "fair treatment."

In an atmosphere of absent or constrained tolerance, former slaves retained
the will to rebuild or invent productive lives, and many remained
close to where they had dreamed of escape while some headed for the North Star once more
looking for work, still haunted by Intolerance, an inescapable bore.
Many failed, but for those who succeeded, in spite of doubts, good Fortune smiled.

Like the crypted songs composed by ancestors burdened with bonded, dismal lots,
music became a respite, a consoler, a balm, an aide in creative plots
for survival or for sanity and hopefulness during long, gloomy days.
Many also found refuge in laughter or in soothing tonics as ways
to camouflage years of psychological pain and grief challenging their worth.

For many who prevailed predicted inferiority or mental misuse
knowledge, discoveries, inventions, creations and milestones erased excuse
that slaves and their posterity too were somehow subhuman creatures, fair game,
or vessels for refuse, denial of education, abuse or defame.
But, skepticism and lack of conviction often die hard, perplexing deaths.

Sadly, some heirs who were the objects of inferiority's claim believed
that they and their forebears were somehow remiss and lacking, so being deceived
displays of heritage languished 'til campaigns and deliberations
swelled and consumed youth who began to express in hair, garb and celebrations
rich, proud and diverse legacies of their ancestral continent, Africa!

Smoldering spirits that had been sheltered by outward acceptance and pretense
were dramatically bared with rhetoric and protest marches in defense
of reality, of Constitutional oaths, and of Freedom's stifled ring.
Among the most forceful voices was the later martyred Martin Luther King.
So passionate and intense were his visions of equality and justice!

Among those opposing the system under attack were friends and descendants
of proponents of the situations that bred the discontent, the hindrance
to Freedoms assumed by those who voted, moved about unbridled and with ease.
Races of all economic groups and all ages joined the struggle for pleas,
requests and demands to rein inequities and to groom Freedom's offerings.

Exposed reality, of true opportunities, of large scale discontent
left some youth, already confused about the aim of an Asian war, to resent
their country's dedication to absolute adherence to declarations.
So, some became devout objectors or joined subculture organizations.
Focus fluttered, but the mid nineteen sixties brought hard-fought, legalized civil rights.

Assassinations and fiery destruction of property stressed the wide range
of the tempestuous atmosphere clouded with concepts about war and change.
But, the nation tried to adjust the climate and right generational wrongs
while perplexing problems hailed among Vietnam soldiers and amidst the throngs
of marchers defying leadership as directions parted the rainbowed groups.

Leadership met returning, bewildered soldiers with complicated replies.
Stunned and coping with emotional stress, veterans sought answers in the eyes
of a seemingly insensitive public reeling from embattled civil rights,
changes intertwined with war and drugs and unfinished social and legal fights.
So, a long, dismal, fragmented, forlorn period of celebration ensued.

The African Americans' journey has taken intricate, daunting paths.
When bars were partly lifted, warriors limped obliquely from wars' aftermaths
knowing well Freedom's limits and seeing vividly Lady Liberty's light;
yet, returning to restrictions and to assumed, reluctant acceptance of their plight.
But, as time passed, Hope's image became less blurry, less latent, less alien.

So long the inhumanity existed; long the minds and bodies endured
lifestyles and conditions with little or no choice after being curtly lured
into an odious incubus that at times seemed hopelessly unending.
But, Faith, a bulwark of unseen possibility, stayed nearby, unbending ….
Finally, Hope's opaque image began to glow … arose composed and uncowed.

Near the dawn of a new century now, Opportunity stands in full view
waiting to embrace the heirs of bonded captives, greeting all who still dare to do
the nurturing, the sacrificing, the creating and the aspiring that yield
the accomplishments and rewards of hopes and dreams that talents and hard work build.
Stains of distress remain, but paths to "The American Dream" are no longer barred.

The posterity of both masters and slaves, not there at the onset of the dark past,
would do well not to perpetuate rancor or evil, nor make dissension last
but go forward having learned to appreciate diversity and to share –
without turmoil, greed or malice – a Land of Opportunity, a place where
Hope survives for the masses whose faces reflect those of the world's continents.

CPSIA information can be obtained
at www.ICGtesting.com
Printed in the USA
BVHW011752170921
616959BV00017B/373